Design for **Aviation**

Gensler

Front cover: Mineta San Jose International Airport
Terminal B Concourse. Inside front cover, from left:
Jomo Kenyatta International Airport, Jackson Hole
Airport. Page i, from left: Incheon International
Airport Terminal 2, John F. Kennedy International
Airport JetBlue Terminal 5. Page ii, from left: Changi
Airport Singapore Terminal 2, SFO Terminal 2.

Contents

OPPOSITE •• Terminal 2 at Changi Airport Singapore features a full canopy over the ticketing hall entry roadway, sheltering travelers from sun and rain. OVERLEAF •• The Virgin America ticketing area at Terminal 2, San Francisco International Airport.

Foreword

An airport is a gateway, a vital link to the larger world. Like the city and region it serves, every airport needs to distinguish itself as an authentic reflection of its community. We design airports with this in mind, seeing them as a vital part of urban infrastructure and equally as desirable places in which to spend time. This is why Gensler believes that the quality of the passenger experience is the real measure of an airport's success. We want our part of the traveler's journey to be a great time, so we design airports that make sense, work beautifully, and convey the real spirit of the place. This translates into higher revenues, increased brand value, and greater civic pride. Travelers seek them out. They remember. And they come back.

Andrew P. Cohen, FAIA
David Gensler
Diane Hoskins, FAIA
Executive Directors, Gensler

Terminal ①
Gates 20-48

International Terminal
Gates A1-A12, G91-G102

Hotel Shuttles
Off-Airport Parking Shuttles
Shared Ride Vans

5

OPPOSITE •• JetBlue's Terminal 5 at New York City's John F. Kennedy International Airport captures the airline's brand by supporting passengers at every step in their journey, from curbside to destination.

Introduction by Allison Arieff

In the past few decades, airports have gone through a series of revolutionary changes. New security regimes, the rise of low-cost airlines, and the growing embrace of technology are steadily shifting the paradigm of what an airport is and how it works. Gensler has been front and center in this revolution. In the US, the firm has built on the implications of 9/11. Globally, it has redefined what a gateway international airport means to some of the world's fastest-growing economies. For both international and domestic airports, Gensler has aggressively leveraged new technologies that deliver a marked improvement in efficiency, flexibility, sustainability, and revenues. Gensler's latest generation of airports and passenger terminals provides a template for what the world requires today of this crucial piece of urban and regional infrastructure.

Enhancing the experience

For almost 40 years, Gensler has made the quality of the passenger experience the focus of its airport work. As Art Gensler, the firm's founder, recalls, "When we first entered the market in 1974, we decided to design airports for the people who use them." Passengers are the ultimate measure of an airport's success, but the quality of the airport experience reflects the efforts of everyone involved in its operation. Gensler airports are designed to help their stakeholders deliver the level of service that air travelers need and expect.

The firm also pays attention to the business issues that an airport's different stakeholders face. "The industry is roiled by new demands, pressures, and innovations, so we design our terminals for constant change," says Gensler's Bill Hooper. "They can't be precious or untouchable, yet they need to be places that passengers appreciate and enjoy." In 2011, *The Street* named JetBlue's Terminal 5 at New York's JFK and San Francisco's Terminal 2—Gensler projects— among America's "six most beautiful terminals." Why does beauty matter, *The Street* asked? "Gorgeous terminals provide a competitive advantage."

ABOVE •• **The translucent and tent-like concourse roof at Palm Springs International Airport is a landmark. OPPOSITE •• Jackson Hole Airport offers a modern take on the craft traditions of the American West.**

Air travelers have choices. Their loyalty means added revenue for airports, airlines, and airport concessions.

Gensler terminals can be found at the airports of cities as diverse as Chennai, Detroit, Incheon, New York, Palm Springs, San Francisco, San Jose, and Singapore. Their repertoire of passenger-serving features directly benefits airports' operational and financial performance. At Incheon, the competition-winning Terminal 2 will shorten travelers' time from airport train to gate to 13 minutes. San Francisco and Singapore redefine the airport shopping experience to embrace the local, while Detroit and Palm Springs are designed to suit their climates and to capture the particular sense of place of their communities.

This starts at the very beginning of the design process. Before planning the modernization of California's Mineta San Jose International Airport, the Gensler team convened a series of community workshops to identify the range of passengers that use the airport. A business traveler rushing to catch an early morning flight to Los Angeles has different needs than a retired couple headed for Hawaii, for example. Because the community felt accommodated in the airport's future, Gensler's plan enjoyed very strong public support.

Defining the next generation of airports

The new generation of airports and terminals that Gensler has pioneered breaks new ground in addressing airport security, leveraging technology effectively and supporting airports and airlines alike as they shift their business models. Gensler airports are redefining the industry in the following ways:

They make the experience enjoyable: Many people find airports hard to navigate. Gensler designs them to be calming and enjoyable rather than stressful and confusing. Air travelers should have a reasonable expectation of what will happen next. This should be intuitively clear without depending on signage. The terminal should anticipate their needs in other ways. For example, Gensler places a recompose zone right after security to let people regroup. Further in, they can shop or have a meal or a drink and still keep an eye on their gates. The amenities that these terminals provide have a level of sophistication that travelers associate with the worlds of hospitality and retail. Not surprisingly, Gensler is a leading designer of hotels, stores, restaurants, and shopping centers.

They address security's implications: It will come as no surprise that security is the source of most air traveler complaints. After 9/11, Gensler gave expert advice to the Transportation Security Administration (TSA) and to numerous airports on addressing TSA's initial requirements. The cost of security falls on the flying public, so the firm has focused on making it faster and more efficient, leveraging technology and,

where possible, reconfiguring the security area to better accommodate screening as part of the larger passenger journey. Terminal 5 at JFK and Terminal 2 at SFO showed how this is done in a US context. Incheon will set a new global standard for gateway airports.

They shift the terminal paradigm: Gensler has consistently led the way in reframing the terminal paradigm in light of the new possibilities created by airport security and technology. In parallel with these changes was the shift that occurred in the airline business following deregulation, ushering in the low-cost airlines. These changes have led many airports to reassert their control of spaces and systems that were previously controlled by the airlines, even as they have ceded security-related areas to TSA. These airports embrace and leverage common use terminal equipment (CUTE) and common use special systems (CUSS), technology that lets them meet the needs of their airline tenants quickly while maintaining unrestricted control of their gates. At John Wayne Airport in Orange County, California, the check-in kiosks are the front end of an airport-run computer system. Travelers there no longer have to find airline-specific kiosks in order to check in.

These changes are affecting the overall design of the terminal. For example, it used to be that the ticket lobby was the airport marquee: every airline wanted the first place on the curb, the splashy back wall, the grand entrance. Today, many passengers arrive at the airport having checked in online. They may pause at a kiosk to print out their boarding passes, but their real destination is security. Once past it, they spend more time on the airside, waiting for their flights. Gensler terminals therefore provide three times more security screening lanes and twice the amount of airside concessions space than the previous generation.

They catch the local style and sensibility: Today's terminals express the local flavor of their locations through architecture, cuisine, materials, and concessions. Homogeneity has given way to localism with a distinct shift toward what's unique to each particular place. T2 at SFO, inspired by San Francisco's iconic Ferry Building Farmer's Market, developed a solution that addressed this desire head-on. Post-security, travelers enter an open, light- and art-filled food and retail concourse. The waiting areas around the gates are capacious and stylishly furnished, with places to work and lots of well-placed outlets to recharge phones, tablets, and laptops.

They serve as regional gateways: International gateway airports like Incheon in South Korea or Changi in Singapore compete to be the connecting point of choice in their region. These hubs anchor national carriers and link their countries' business interests with their markets—and vice versa. A gateway airport provides access to the metropolis it serves and makes it easy and efficient for travelers to make short visits and then move on to other places.

They embrace sustainability at every level: Sustainability is a key driver of Gensler's airport practice. SFO Terminal 2, for example, is America's first LEED Gold certified terminal. The firm take a holistic approach to sustainability. "Cutting the time airplanes spend taxiing by just 90 seconds at a busy domestic

ABOVE •• **The iconic entry canopy of Terminal 2 at Changi Airport Singapore is the image of choice to represent Singapore's leadership as a global hub.**

airport like LaGuardia can save $4 or $5 million a year in operating costs," says Gensler's Keith Thompson. Airports and airlines, sensitive about their carbon footprints, are big advocates for sustainable practices. Terminal 2 at Incheon pushes the envelope by considering every aspect of sustainability, aiming both to reduce energy and water consumption and

increase building performance. The self-supporting translucent roof brings natural light into the terminal with a minimum of structural columns, saving materials and providing large interior spaces that need almost no artificial lighting in the daytime. The terminal integrates the intercity trains that link it to Seoul and other regional destinations, placing the trains' arrival point as close as possible to the rest of the passenger journey to save significant time as people hurry to their gates.

They serve as destinations: Incheon's Terminal 2 breaks new ground in providing a self-contained international conference center that air travelers can access without having to leave the airport precinct. Gensler-designed airports in Europe, Africa, and Asia

emphasize their long-term potential to serve as "airport cities" that can attract an array of compatible uses that value airport proximity. With seamless transit to, from, and within the airport—a concept that Gensler proposed in its modernization plan for California's Mineta San Jose International Airport 10 years ago—the airport emerges as true destination. More than a gateway, it can serve as a meeting point between the metropolis it serves and the wider world. Airports usually have land to spare for development. Hotels, conference centers, and other uses complement an airport's primary function and help activate it as a 24/7 destination.

They stand the test of time: Gensler's renovation of SFO's T2 was its second encounter with the 57-year-

OPPOSITE ●● Airports use people movers to connect their terminals as an accessible whole. **ABOVE, TOP ●●** This CityCenter, Las Vegas station features a lightweight cable-structure roof. **OVERLEAF ●●** View of the main façade of the Terminal B Concourse at California's Mineta San Jose International Airport.

old building. A 1983 renovation turned the former central terminal into SFO's first international terminal. A generation later, Gensler returned it to domestic service. As long-lived structures, terminals need to facilitate ongoing maintenance and modernization. Gensler builds in maximum flexibility to meet the future needs that airports can't always anticipate.

Incheon's new Terminal 2 wraps the passenger journey in a high-performance building envelope. Easy to keep clean and maintain, the translucent, self-supporting roof structure encloses large, column-free spaces. This will let the airport fit out the interior with lightweight, modular furnishings that can be reconfigured and refreshed easily in the future without requiring the time and expense of a major renovation.

Designing the future of airports

In the first decade of the 21st century, Gensler gained a reputation for solving the dilemmas that 9/11 and the changing airline business posed for US airports. JetBlue's T5 and SFO's T2 are widely known examples of how domestic passenger terminals in the US should perform, while smaller airports like Portland, Maine, and Jackson, Wyoming, have redefined that category. Moving toward 2020, Gensler's growing portfolio of international gateway terminals is similarly helping to shift the global airport paradigm.

What is striking about Gensler's airport portfolio is its diversity. It's not surprising that an airport in Lagos starts with different premises than one in Silicon Valley, but Gensler takes even subtle differences seriously, building on the opportunities they provide for innovation. Inflected with a true local flavor, the airports Gensler has designed around the world have true sense of place. What could be more 21st-century?

Allison Arieff is editor of *The Urbanist* and writes for the *New York Times* and *The Atlantic Cities*. Based in San Francisco, she is a former editor of *Dwell*.

Redefining the airport

Transforming the industry, one airport at a time

Today's well-designed airport has disproportional brand value. Few modern buildings are called on to express the spirit and aspirations of the communities and airlines that commission them. And few combine such an experiential design challenge with the need to solve functional and technical problems. The following case studies, the work of Gensler's Aviation & Transportation practice, illustrate how our designers make the experience of air travel a pleasure again. They demonstrate how our integrated approach to airport planning and design is transforming the industry by delivering the performance that airports need to compete effectively in today's fast-paced, highly competitive world.

Incheon International Airport

Terminal 2
Incheon, South Korea

In brief

A new passenger terminal that doubles the size of South Korea's gateway airport. The terminal cuts train-to-flight times and makes Incheon East Asia's best airport for shoppers.

Incheon International Airport is the largest airport in South Korea. One of the world's busiest airports, Incheon is highly rated by the air travelers it serves. Terminal 2 will double the airport's size while making the quality of the passenger experience even better. This reflects the client's goal of securing Incheon's place as East Asia's leading airport hub, a gateway destination for international travelers. In addition to a new international terminal, the airport's expansion program includes a second control tower, a train station, parking facilities, and an adjoining hotel and conference center. Terminal 2's translucent roof tempers outdoor air as it lights the interior. Departing passengers need very little time to reach their gates from the airport trains, unless they pause to shop.

OPPOSITE •• Terminal 2 is organized for fast, efficient handling of airplane traffic. It features a park-like conference center and, inside the terminal, a vast shopping center. Both cater to air travelers who make the airport itself their destination.

Gensler teamed with Heerim Architects & Planners to win Terminal 2 in an international design competition. The expansion reflects the airport's determination to be a leading gateway hub in East Asia, connecting international travelers to other cities in the region. One of the important drivers of the design is that Incheon Airport serves as a major shopping destination for travelers from across East Asia. Some come only to shop, never leaving the airport. Terminal 2's 100,000-square-meter concessions area is about 25 percent of the total space, split evenly between airside and landside. It is designed to create an unparalleled, world-class shopping experience.

Terminal 2 includes a range of sustainable strategies. Photovoltaic cells integrated with the building skin and on-site wind turbines provide renewable sources of electricity, augmented by pressure-plate electric-power generators on airport taxiways and roads. The building envelope and HVAC systems work together to ensure comfort. High-performance glazing brings natural daylight to the interior with minimal glare. The terminal roof buffers the interior from the changing climate. In winter, the heat loss is from the roof's

ABOVE •• Terminal 2 addresses every aspect of airport performance, from the efficiency of airline operations to the high standard of the passenger experience. **OVERLEAF** •• The self-supporting roof creates large-volume interiors, like the rail station, with abundant daylight and very few columns.

Design fact

Concessions area at Terminal 2

100k sq m

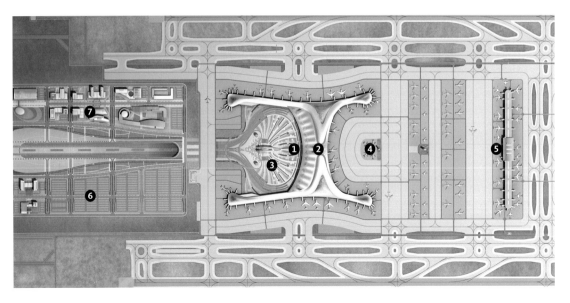

Master Plan

1: Railroad station 2
2: Passenger terminal
3: Front passenger terminal
4: Control tower
5: Existing Concourse A
6: Long-term parking
7: Adjacent facility

interstitial cavity rather than from the inside of the building. In summer, the sun's heat is absorbed by the same cavity. The roof structure is only 30.5 centimeters thick above the concessions hall, letting dappled light filter through to add interest to the shopping experience. The entire terminal and portions of the concourse are shaded by solar-shading devices and roof overhangs. The building skin is designed so that outside air or exhaust air can form a thermal buffer, greatly reducing energy consumption. The unique architectural forms in combination with materials such as glass and Teflon create a pleasant and energy-efficient environment.

Although it is almost twice as big as Terminal 1, the new terminal is designed for clarity. Passengers arriving by car or train can clearly see the ticketing hall, ticketing counters, security locations, and the people mover. The arrival and departure levels align with and are connected by the people mover, allowing seamless transfer between the terminals and reducing wait times for transfers. The column-free space of the departure hall is completely open, so navigation is intuitive. Ticketed passengers have the option to check in with ticketing agents or to self-check.

Following check-in, passengers move through the immigration hall for processing before reaching the duty-free concessions hall. This column-free volume has a clear span of 91.5 meters, allowing unimpeded sight lines. Shoppers reach their gates on the people mover, directly accessible from the concessions hall.

Arriving passengers enter a customs hall, which is located above the double-height baggage hall. Once processed, they descend to retrieve their luggage before entering the meeters-and-greeters area. To give travelers an immediate sense of place, the choice of materials and designs in these spaces, including the signage and graphics, draws on textures and colors that invoke Korean culture and traditions. The flooring in the airport, for example, uses locally quarried granite and traditional Korean wood.

A planned 300-room hotel and conference center will connect by a bridge to the arrival and departure halls. Spanning the parking garage, it will be set within a garden park designed to reflect the ecology of Incheon Island, including the ebb and flow of the tide. The terminal's innovative thin-shell structural system integrates form and structure. The ticketing hall's exterior curtain wall

Terminal 2: Key Innovations

1: The rail station's location cuts the walking distance from trains to gates.

2: The rail station has direct access to Terminal 2's arrival and departure levels.

3: The automated people mover is convenient to immigration and airline clubs and lounges.

4: The self-supporting roof saves weight and brings daylighting into the departure hall.

5: The roof creates an exceptionally spacious departure hall with relatively few columns.

is mullion-free, using a point-supported cable stay system. The space-frame roof structure uses light baffles to diffuse and soften the natural light. The roof panels form patterns that are recognizably drawn from Korean precedents. Providing rail service directly to the terminal helps make it accessible. The rail station's close-in location allows passengers to move quickly from the trains to the gates.

Terminal 2 fulfills the Incheon Airport Corporation's mandate to use sustainable development to maintain its position as a leading international gateway airport in East Asia, responding proactively to future changes in aviation and airports by using state-of-the-art technology and flexible planning.

OPPOSITE •• The ticketing hall uses demountable components that can be quickly upgraded without major construction. OVERLEAF •• The main entry to Terminal 2's departure level and ticketing hall.

Changi Airport Singapore

Terminal 2 Renovation
Singapore

In brief

The full modernization of Terminal 2 at Changi Airport Singapore, renovated by Gensler after only 10 years in service to maintain the world-class quality for which the airport is famous.

Changi Airport Singapore has long ranked among the top airports in the world, but new competitors in the region are an ongoing threat to its high standing. This led Changi to stage an international competition to renew and upgrade Terminal 2, which had only been in operation for a decade. Gensler and its Singapore partner, RSP Architects Planners & Engineers, were chosen. The result is a virtually new terminal—with an iconic new entrance canopy, an upgraded ticketing lobby, and vastly expanded passenger amenities that convey Changi's determination to be the international airport of choice for a new generation of travelers.

OPPOSITE •• Terminal 2's renovation added a deep weather canopy that protects travelers from even the heaviest rainfall. The canopy has become an icon for Changi Airport Singapore as a whole.

One driver for Changi's decision to update Terminal 2 was to upgrade its appearance and functioning and realize its full commercial potential. Increasing the passenger-handling capacity was a key objective, affording the opportunity to bring every aspect of the passenger's experience to a best-in-class standard. The existing terminal suffered from the lack of an effective shelter from tropical rainstorms at the curbside drop-off for departing passengers. Taking inspiration from bamboo and other native plants, Gensler designed a cantilevered canopy that protects travelers from the elements while allowing for increased natural light and views. The use of light steel members with translucent glass panels brightens what was formerly a dark and forbidding entrance.

Arriving passengers enter through the near-transparent front façade into a brightly sky-lit lobby, crossing over interior bridges that span a tropical garden rising from the arrival level one floor below. This theme is recalled as travelers enter the departure hall, where the sweeping ceiling of brightly lit glass panels forms a rhythmic pattern of leaf shapes. Additional daylight is brought deep into the terminal via a louvered skylight that runs the length of the terminal at the threshold to the immigration processing area. (The window wall was developed in collaboration with Hugh Dutton Associates, Paris.)

Terminal 2 enhances and maximizes the commercial potential of shopping and food and beverage operations. Gensler remodeled and expanded the existing retail space to create a stylish, two-level retail setting organized around a series of gardens. Upscale retailers that once shared shelf space with midpriced goods in a generic retail space are now housed in individual boutiques designed to showcase their brands.

Gensler developed storefront design guidelines to ensure cohesiveness and created new space for restaurants on the airside of the terminal. The soaring, glass-enclosed extension, 30,000 square feet in total, rises above the terminal's apron. It generates additional revenue for the airport and provides departing travelers with a gallery where they can enjoy panoramic views of the runways and planes.

Site Plan

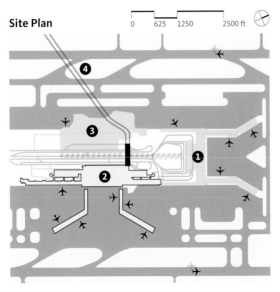

0   625   1250   2500 ft

Performance facts

Annual passenger-handling capacity	First-year increase in retail sales
22 m	**67**%

OPPOSITE •• Terminal 2 provides casual settings for waiting passengers to work. BELOW •• As befits the "garden city," the plantscape of Singapore is an important design element inside the terminal.

1:   Terminal 1
2:   Terminal 2
3:   Terminal 3
4:   MRT (subway) connection

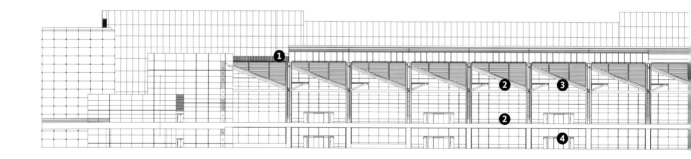

BELOW •• The 820-foot-long canopy gives strong
visual interest to Terminal 2's curbside entrance.

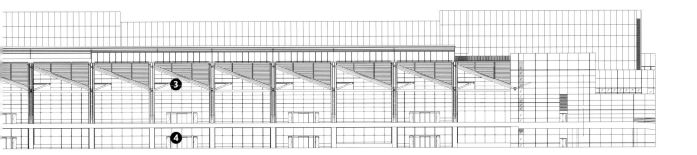

Landside Arrivals/Departures Elevation

1: Exterior canopy
2: Glass curtain wall
3: Departures entry vestibules
4: Arrivals exit vestibules

BELOW •• View of Terminal 2. OPPOSITE •• The two-story entry and bridges. OVERLEAF •• View of the curbside entry from one of the entry bridges.

Section of Arrivals/Departures

1: Skylight
2: Louvers
3: Canopy
4: Teak columns
5: Curtain wall
6: Arrivals
7: Departures
8: Planting
9: Bridge to departure hall
10: Entry vestibule

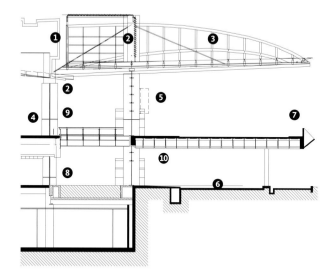

John F. Kennedy International Airport

JetBlue Terminal 5
Queens, New York, USA

In brief

Among the first designed to post-9/11 security requirements, Terminal 5 exemplifies the JetBlue brand. With 26 gates, T5 is JFK's busiest, with more than 30 percent of its passenger traffic.

One of the first new US passenger terminals designed to reflect post-9/11 security measures, Terminal 5 (T5) also serves as an extension of JetBlue's successful brand and business model. Inviting and amenity-filled, it provides a world-class ambience without costly and unnecessary grandeur. Wrapped around the iconic TWA Terminal, a 1960s landmark, T5's crisp modernity emphasizes the efficiency and comfort of air travel. The 26-gate terminal is JFK's busiest, handling more than 30 percent of the airport's passenger traffic. To minimize flight delays, the gates are spaced for faster plane turnaround. With 20 security screen lanes, T5 moves travelers quickly through security to an airside experience that begins with the popular marketplace, offering 57 different shops and restaurants.

OPPOSITE •• **Terminal 5 is located directly behind the iconic TWA Terminal at JFK. While the buildings are connected by a bridging walkway, T5 reflects a 21st-century sensibility that clearly differentiates it.**

41

JetBlue's sleek new T5 at JFK sets a new standard for passenger comfort and operational efficiency among low-cost carriers. T5's curved rooflines gesture to its famous neighbor, Eero Saarinen's TWA Terminal, a symbol of the early jet age. Gensler designed the 635,000-square-foot T5 to handle 250 flights per day or 20 million passengers per year, doubling JetBlue's operating capacity at JFK to a level equivalent to the total annual passenger load at New York's LaGuardia Airport. T5 is built for 21st-century air travel, with self-service options for passengers and an easily navigated, 20-lane security checkpoint. Soft rubber flooring and wide family lanes speed the process. Just beyond security, a 225-foot-long bench wall lets travelers pause and regroup.

ABOVE •• The sweeping curbside entry of JetBlue Terminal 5. OPPOSITE •• Inside the ticketing hall, a light-filled space that moves passengers quickly through check-in to 20 security screening lanes.

T5 combines exposed structural steel and curved clerestory windows to create a light-filled ticketing hall and airside marketplace. On the landside, T5 uses the TWA Terminal's "wing tubes" to bridge to the older building, anticipating its eventual reuse. T5 has the flexibility to adapt readily to new check-in and security technology. Wayfinding relies on a clear plan and such visual cues as blue walls and directional ramps. To expedite the preflight experience, a cutting-edge, automated in-line baggage system takes checked bags directly from the ticketing area through screening to the aircraft and can sort 400 bags per hour. An opening at the departure level brings light to the six-carousel baggage-claim area. Each carousel provides a generous 180 feet of luggage display.

OPPOSITE •• The ticketing hall. ABOVE, TOP •• The 20-lane security area. ABOVE, BOTTOM •• A place to pause before heading to the gates. OVERLEAF •• On the way, passengers encounter the marketplace. A ring of monitors connects them to other travelers.

Gates 1 to 7 ➜

On the airside, the spacious, light-filled, 55,000-square-foot marketplace offers 35 specialty stores and 22 cafés, lounges, and restaurants. T5's 26 boarding gates are located in three concourses that are organized around the marketplace. Each concourse has lounge and traditional seating, a customer-service zone, and quiet visual paging. The gates are close to the marketplace, so passengers won't feel rushed while they shop or get some food, but there are also touch-screen monitors they can use to order food and drinks for gate-side delivery, an airline industry first. (More space between gates lets JetBlue turn planes around in 30 minutes, 40 percent faster than average.)

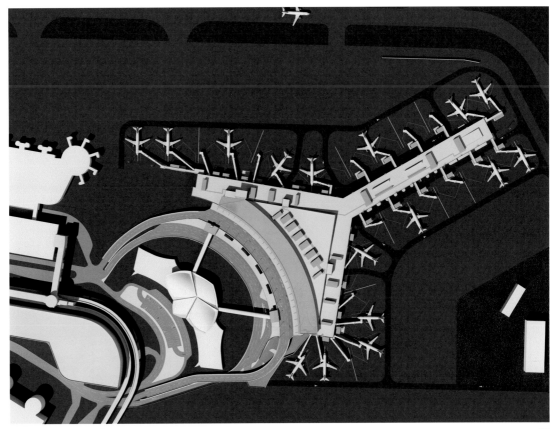

San Francisco International Airport

Terminal 2 Renovation
San Francisco, California, USA

In brief

Gensler's second renovation of a 1952 building resulted in a LEED Gold terminal that is a global benchmark for tipping passengers' experience toward hospitality and a true sense of place.

First built in 1952, then expanded by Gensler in 1981 as SFO's first international terminal, Terminal 2 (T2) was reinvented by Gensler in a design-build partnership with Turner Construction. The 640,000-square-foot, 14-gate terminal opened in 2011 with American and Virgin America as its anchors, gaining acclaim locally and globally. T2's sense of place is distinctively San Franciscan. Travelers can see the bay and hills through generous windows and skylights, and they can also experience the work of local artists (curated by the San Francisco Arts Commission) and food made from locally sourced organic ingredients. The success of T2 is in the details, large and small, that add up to a memorable setting. As San Francisco Mayor Ed Lee put it, "We felt like we'd walked into a five-star hotel."

OPPOSITE ●● Ticketing areas are tucked in the sides of Terminal 2's departure hall. Local artists, curated by the San Francisco Arts Commission, accentuate the visual dynamism of the space. **OVERLEAF** ●● The transparency of the completely rebuilt departure-level entry reveals the space and brings in light.

An integral part of Gensler's T2 design strategy was to give passengers a sense of comfort and control at all of T2's touchpoints. Take the concessions area: San Francisco is a set of closeknit neighborhoods connected by sky and views, so Gensler's team evoked that sense of place within the terminal. Skylights and a dramatic ceiling installation by a local artist, Janet Echelman, draw attention up and out to a dramatic view of the airfield. The place feels special, reflecting the airport's goal of making travelers feel good again.

Gensler was deliberate in not filling up every inch of the space. Computer load tests were done to ensure that the generous use of open space wouldn't create bottlenecks at peak periods. A more comfortable, less stressful environment is achieved with architectural moves that improve visibility. Passengers can readily see where to go next, which helps minimize stress.

Once past the security checkpoint, the traveler's voyage becomes about the options he or she has for spending time before departure. From Gensler's post-security recompose area, passengers have great

ABOVE, TOP •• Natural light is a consistent element in T2's design. **ABOVE, BOTTOM** •• The boarding area mixes uses and seating, all close to gates. **OPPOSITE** •• The recompose area just past security lets people pause and put themselves back together.

Gates 50-59

Departure-Level Plan

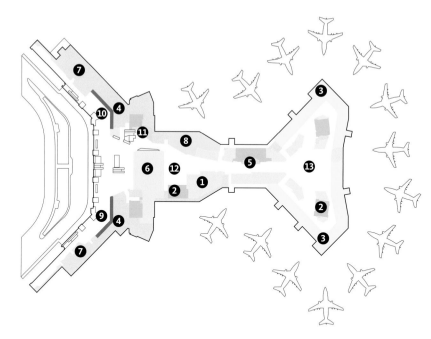

1: **Concessions and retail**
2: **Restrooms**
3: **Gate lounges**
4: **Ticketing/check-in**
5: **Museum displays**
6: **Security screening**
7: **Back of house**
8: **Airline club**
9: **Virgin America**
10: **American Airlines**
11: **Meet and greet**
12: **Recompose zone**
13: **Concessions court**

views of retail and concession options—the wide and open storefronts are invitations to come in and explore. Having no long corridors ensures a welcoming experience. Passengers can stroll by the shops and restaurants instead of rushing to the boarding area. The arrangement of retail spaces in the departure lounge is intentionally decentralized to avoid a "food court look" and give passengers a sense of discovery. There are lots of places to linger here: passengers can savor an espresso, browse the locally owned bookstore, enjoy a meal on the indoor terrace of the Lark Creek Grill, or take in one of SFO's renowned museum exhibits, all with their gate still visible.

The airside of T2 feels very much a part of the city it serves. The eclectic, largely locally owned retail mix was inspired by San Francisco's historic Ferry Building Farmer's Market, and many of the carefully curated restaurants and stores are offshoots of local businesses. Their inclusion here creates a sense of place. Travelers long accustomed to being disoriented by the overwhelming sameness of most airport terminals will appreciate this more contextual approach.

OPPOSITE, TOP •• The airside is an expansive, light-filled space that offers travelers a range of options as they wait for their flights. **OPPOSITE, BOTTOM ••** The concessions emphasize the Bay Region in their dining and shopping choices.

Sustainability is a given in San Francisco, one of America's greenest cities, and T2 is the first airport terminal in the US to be certified LEED Gold. Gensler's green decisions reflected potential energy savings and the positive impact of each measure on the passengers. T2's retail tenants, for example, had 16 LEED points to deliver on. They were asked to explain their approach to sustainability beyond recycling and the use of low-VOC materials. Gensler's development of comprehensive storefront sustainability guidelines, and its ongoing collaboration with T2's retail tenants as they built out their spaces, resulted in storefronts that, as one retail tenant put it, "raise the bar for all future work at SFO."

EIGHT LANES OF SECURITY •• Faster security means less stress; then passengers get to decompress! Security is as easy as it can be; then there's a place to recompose. The next moves on the airside are clearly and attractively visible.

SUSTAINABLE COMMITMENT •• T2's sustainable strategy plays out in small ways and large. Passengers can fill their water bottles after security. They can also learn green practices and bask in a healthy, efficient LEED Gold terminal.

FIVE STARS •• San Francisco Mayor Ed Lee said of T2, "We felt like we'd walked into a five-star hotel." The design is influenced by hospitality, with a Bay Area flavor and family-friendly ambience. That level of thoughtfulness extends to every aspect of T2.

GATEWAY TO THE REGION •• T2 is the Bay Area's warm welcome and its fond farewell. It features world-class art by local artists, wonderful bay views, and quick access to regional trains to San Francisco, Oakland, and San Jose.

Green fact

T2's annual reduction in greenhouse gases

1,667 tons

Performance fact

Passengers served, first year in operation

3.2 million

Security is one reason why T2 is widely seen as a quantum leap in passenger comfort. Gensler took a new look at the security area, providing more points of entry—a total of eight passenger lanes—and very clear wayfinding. The result is a security screening process that works efficiently and is easy to navigate.

"This is one of the few terminals in America where you arrive and think it's going to be a great day," Virgin America Chairman Sir Richard Branson said on T2's opening day. "Fun" and "enjoyment" aren't words that people normally apply to airports, but T2 is changing that. Says Virgin America Design Director Jesse McMillin, "We all went in with the feeling that T2, located in San Francisco, begs to be revolutionary."

ABOVE •• T2's airside space is layered to give people a constant sense of what's on offer without making those offerings feel obtrusive. Wherever they are in the space, waiting passengers are always aware of what's happening at the gate. OVERLEAF •• T2's open plan makes it unusually clear and easy to navigate.

↑ ✈ **Gates 50-59**

Restrooms

61

Mineta San Jose International Airport

Terminal B Concourse
San Jose, California, USA

In brief

Part of Gensler's modernization master plan for the airport, the Terminal B Concourse combines Silicon Valley's spirit of innovation with San Jose's Hispanic roots and traditions.

The expansion of Mineta San Jose International Airport recognizes its role as Silicon Valley's gateway. The now-completed program was guided by Gensler's updated master plan, which used the full potential of the airport's tightly packed site—hemmed in by two freeways, the Guadalupe River, and existing development. The airport modernization program includes a new central terminal (Terminal B), a consolidated car rental garage, and an improved roadway. Gensler's Terminal B Concourse sets the stage for the expanded airport for arriving passengers. Enclosing a 1,600-foot-long promenade, the building exploits new design methods and materials to achieve a dynamic appearance suited to Silicon Valley's innovative spirit.

OPPOSITE ●● The concourse's curved, translucent roof, draped with a mesh-like shade fabric, recalls the canvas sunscreens that protect Latin American street markets. **OVERLEAF ●●** The dynamic façade of the 1,600-foot-long concourse exploits digital design tools and fabrication methods.

63

Gensler revisited and updated the master plan for Mineta San Jose International Airport's modernization using a scenario planning process that was carried out in a series of community workshops. The design team posited a range of passenger types and personalities. These "avatars" helped illustrate how the airport would be typically used by its different constituents. This resulted in strong community backing for the plan and clear design direction for its components.

The undulating façade of the concourse is inspired by imagery drawn from San Jose's anchor position in Silicon Valley. From the double helix of the design team's original concept, the building developed into a potent symbol of the region's relentless innovation. Fittingly, three-dimensional design software was used to create elements like the asymmetrical roof form, hovering over sail-like, perforated aluminum screens that appear to peel away from the building's core.

Downtown San Jose is still organized around a traditional *paseo*—a sunny pedestrian street that serves as an armature for community life. Within a five-block stretch, residents and visitors can experience the civic, convention, cultural, retail, sports,

entertainment, and educational settings, making the *paseo* a regional destination. Gensler applied this idea to the concourse. The 1,600-foot-long promenade is like a Latin American market street. Sunlight coming in through the curved, transparent roof is shaded by fritted-pattern glass with a draped layer of fabric underneath, recalling the canvas awnings of market stalls. To serve passengers waiting for their flights, the 100,900-square-foot promenade is lined with shops, cafés, and restaurants. Stopping points with restrooms are provided every 300 feet, designed to a hospitality standard of quality and finish.

A commitment to limit the airport's environmental impact greatly influenced the design of the new concourse and its operating systems. Interior daylight is provided by the skylights and a full-height glass façade with integral light shelves, facing the airfield. Digital controls balance artificial and natural light to reduce energy use. Further energy gains are realized using a low-velocity displacement ventilation system in the public areas. The shape of the building complements the performance of this system by allowing hot air to stratify in the high ceiling area and be vented to the outside.

Site Plan

0   300   600   1200 ft

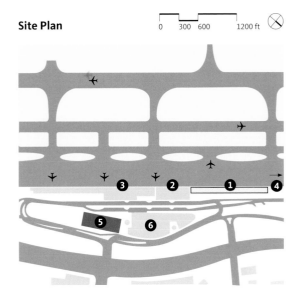

1: Terminal B
   Concourse
2: Terminal B, Phase 1
3: Terminal B, Phase 2

4: Terminal A
5: Parking garage
6: Rental car center

OPPOSITE •• A rendered airside view of the Terminal B Concourse, showing its roof pattern. A full-height curtain wall provides additional natural light and views of the hills that surround Silicon Valley.

Green facts

Energy savings vs. California Title 24	Water savings vs. conventional
14%	**20**%

Landside Elevation

1: Perforated aluminum
2: Staggered insulated metal panels with integrated lights
3: Blue glass/aluminum plate
4: Plaster base
5: Insulated metal "outer skin"
6: Perforated aluminum *brise soleil* façade

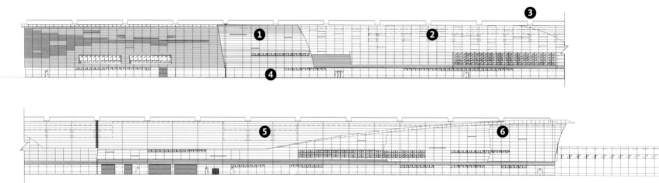

Typical Section

1: Mechanical
2: Skylight
3: Boarding area
4: Light mast
5: Fixed bridge
6: Ground service area/ equipment
7: Operations
8: Utility/baggage
9: Retail/concessions
10: Insulated metal
11: Profile metal

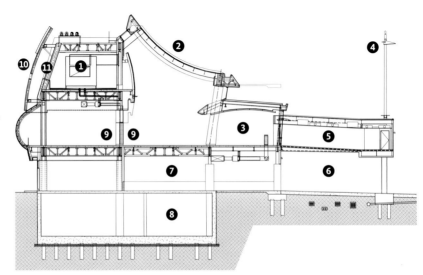

Denver International Airport

South Terminal Redevelopment Program
Denver, Colorado, USA

In brief

A new rail line linking Denver and its airport will cut travel times to 30 minutes. In response, DIA is adding a transit center with a 500-room hotel, a conference center, and a major public plaza.

Serving more than 50 million passengers annually, Denver International Airport (DIA) is Colorado's primary economic engine and one of the world's busiest airports. To make this civic destination more easily accessible, Denver is building a 23-mile Regional Transit District East rail line connecting DIA and Union Station, the city's regional transit hub, to provide reliable, 30-minute service between them. DIA in turn is building a transit center, a 500-room hotel and conference center, and a public plaza that will serve as a regional landmark at the airport and provide a critical link between DIA's existing Jeppesen Terminal complex and the future South Terminal. Initially engaged to design the hotel and conference center only, Gensler is now responsible for the entire new development, including the transit center.

OPPOSITE •• Travelers are sheltered by a translucent archway roof as they approach the hotel from the plaza. **OVERLEAF** •• The new transit center complex gives Denver's airport a city-facing front door.

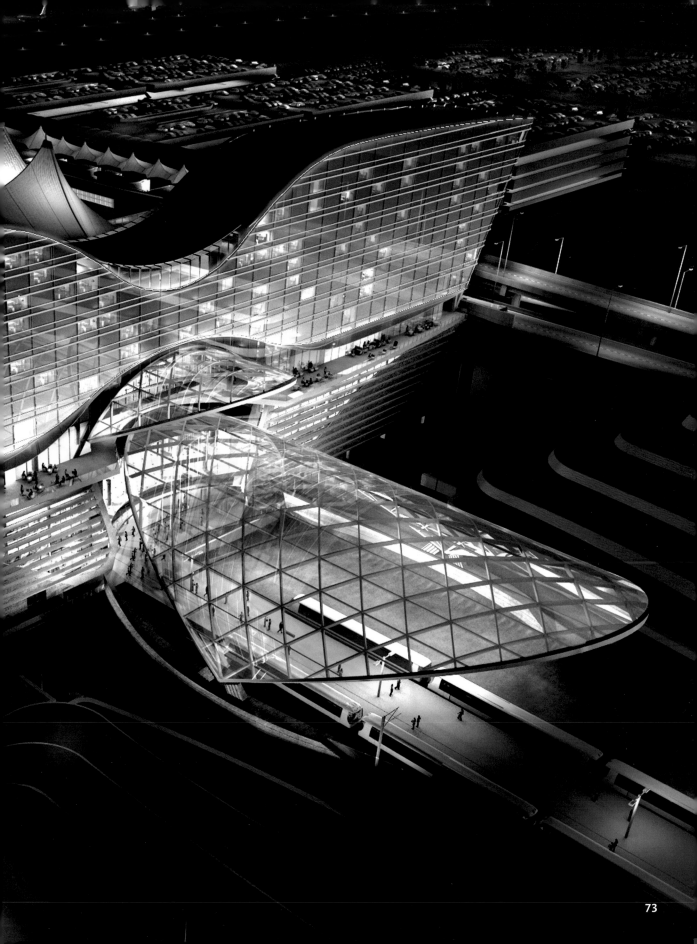

The new building brings dynamic urban amenities to DIA, yet takes its formal inspiration from the existing terminal and the surrounding landscape. The 14-story structure is anchored by a sandstone plinth housing a four-track train hall, a two-story conference center, and arrivals and security processing. The hotel rises up from the plinth. The hotel roof dips at the center to form a "saddle" that defers to the Jeppesen Terminal's iconic roofline and frames the public plaza.

Lined with local concessions, the plaza forms the civic heart of the project—a venue for public events that is equally accessible to air travelers and the community. This generous gathering place gets added prominence from the signature design element of the complex. This is a 250-foot-long canopy that cantilevers beyond

ABOVE, TOP •• The pool sits within the hotel roof's "saddle." **ABOVE, BOTTOM ••** The hotel's sky lobby. **OPPOSITE, TOP ••** A view of the hotel and public plaza from the airport side. **OPPOSITE, BOTTOM ••** The cityside view of the hotel and transit center.

the building in the direction of the existing terminal. The canopy is mirrored on the south side of the building, where its 300-foot-long counterpart serves as the train hall's vaulted roof. This expansive volume creates a grand sense of arrival for passengers, which the hotel tower—rising above them—accentuates. The transit center's elegant design is matched by

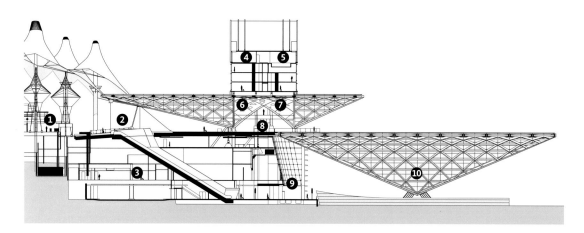

Transit Center Section

1: **Existing terminals**
2: **Plaza**
3: **Service operations**

4: **Fitness center**
5: **Pool**
6: **Sky lobby**

7: **Hotel check-in**
8: **Plaza overlook**
9: **Train hall**

10: **Train canopy**

its robust infrastructure, which includes baggage tug drives and people movers that run below the public plaza to connect the terminals. For passengers arriving by train, six ticketing and baggage check counters, 24 e-ticket kiosks, and 10 security lanes expedite the arrivals process.

The $500 million expansion reinforces DIA as a world-class aviation hub and strengthens its synergy with the Denver metroplex. When the South Terminal Redevelopment Program is completed in 2015, it will generate some 1,000 new jobs and $2 million in annual tax revenue and give DIA a transit-served public entry with a civic presence worthy of the American West's gateway city.

OPPOSITE •• The transit center gives passengers a quick and direct way to travel between Denver's Union Station, a regional transit hub, and DIA. It also gives the airport a city-facing public entry.

Chennai International Airport

International and Domestic Terminals
Chennai Metroplex, India

India's third-busiest airport, Chennai International is the gateway to India's sixth-largest city and its region. Anticipating a steady increase in passenger volume, the Airports Authority of India (AAI) held a limited international competition for the design of a new domestic terminal that would serve as the model for the airport's expansion. Gensler, Frederic Schwartz Architects, and the Creative Group won with an iconic, 21st-century facility with a regional sense of place. The AAI subsequently expanded the commission to include a new international terminal, similar in design to the domestic terminal, and a roadway and pedestrian link among all four terminals. Together, the two new terminals will increase the airport's annual volume by 12 million passengers, twice its current capacity.

In brief

Gensler's first aviation project in India expands the gateway airport to the country's south. The program includes a domestic and international terminal, to be completed in 2012 and 2013.

OPPOSITE •• **View of the check-in hall entry and roadways. The roof canopy helps shelter travelers. Landscape elements throughout the development create a garden setting that reflects the region.**
ABOVE •• **View of the check-in hall interior. Free of columns, its openness allows maximum flexibility.**

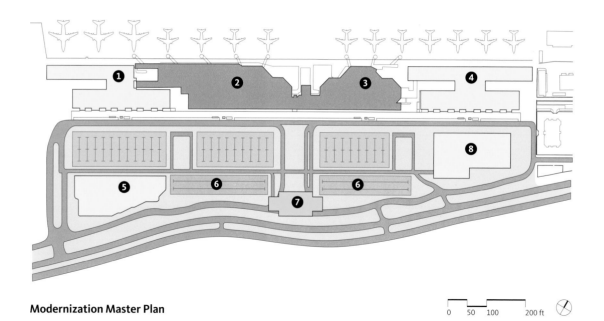

Modernization Master Plan

0   50   100   200 ft

1: **New international terminal**
2: **Existing international terminal**
3: **Existing domestic terminal**
4: **New domestic terminal**
5: **Electrical substation**
6: **Taxi parking**
7: **New Metro station**
8: **Multilevel parking**

Designed as a prototype for the next generation of government-operated airports in India, Chennai's new terminals are organized as parallel landside and airside wings joined by a central security screening hall. Each wing's free-span volume is defined by an arcade of curved trusses that touch the floor as triangulated pylons. The resulting structural-bay module can be extended in the future to add space in a cost-effective way. The structural system brings daylighting to the interior through broad glass curtain walls, protected on the south façade by a deep cantilever.

Between the wings, two tropical gardens, an acre each, bring the South Indian landscape into the terminal. The gardens' reflecting pools and cisterns store overflow rainwater funneled from the roofs, a sustainable source of irrigation in the dry season. Contoured to maximize rainwater harvesting, the roofs' elliptical openings let rainwater flow into cisterns below, creating a rain screen. The natural elements are complemented by bronze and local granite to tie the airport to Chennai's culture and history. The presence of nature creates a uniquely South Indian atmosphere and helps orient passengers in the terminal.

OPPOSITE, TOP •• Airside overview of the seven-gate domestic terminal with the hold-room concourse in the foreground. **OPPOSITE, BOTTOM** •• Interior view of the hold-room concourse and its boarding area.

Arriving passengers first encounter the gardens while crossing them on midlevel bridges. Even the parking garage roof is landscaped. At every point, gardens and green spaces draw travelers toward the next stage of their journey. This invigorating sequence evokes the beauty and vitality of the growing city and region.

The concessions are centrally located to give shoppers views into the gardens and into the hold room proper so that the boarding area is always in view. With its distinctive red walls, the core creates two different zones within the hold-room concourse: a concessions area that is an active retail zone, and a boarding area that is a quiet zone for work or preflight relaxation.

Airport Terminal Courtyard

1: Ticketing gate
2: Departing passengers
3: Arriving passengers
4: Lush planting strips
5: Vertical gardens
6: Pedestrian bridge

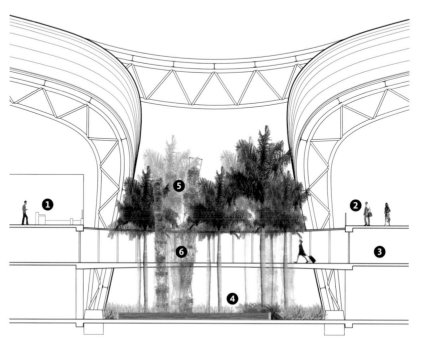

Design fact

Total garden area per terminal

3,400 sq ft

OPPOSITE •• View of one of the two courtyard gardens that are a special feature of the terminal. Visible from all three levels, the gardens draw on the vegetation of Chennai and its region to give travelers an authentic sense of place. **OVERLEAF** •• At dusk and at night, the terminal's transparency makes it a visible landmark for arriving passengers.

Axonometric of the Courtyard Gardens

1: **The gardens:** Each is 1,700 square feet in area.

2: **Planting strips:** These create a colorful patchwork at the base of the courtyard.

3: **Water collection and storage system:** The terminal roof collects rainwater, which is stored in reflective pools for future irrigation use.

4: **Palm grove:** Palm trees provide a shade canopy.

5: **Vertical gardens:** Perennials' vibrant colors are visible from all three levels of the terminal.

6: **Building courtyard composite:** The symbiotic relationship between the building and the garden enriches the passenger experience.

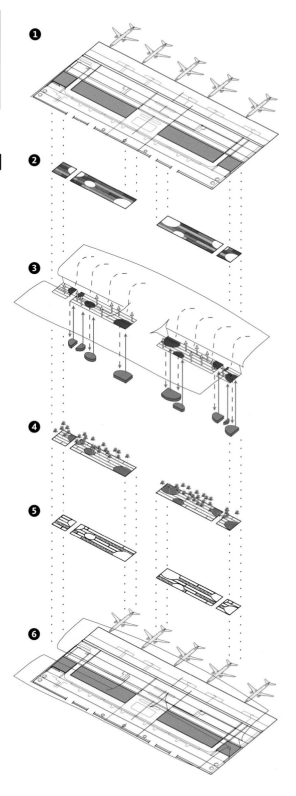

Harbin Taiping International Airport

Terminal 2 and Transportation Center
Taiping, China

In brief

Gensler's proposal for a new terminal and transportation center for Harbin's airport is designed to support the growth of tourism in a city known for its winter sports and festivals.

Harbin Taiping Airport was already a major hub in China's northeast when Gensler and CSADI jointly proposed its expansion to serve growing national and international passenger demand. Transit access is crucial to Harbin's ambitions for tourism, including the 2022 Winter Olympics. The airport is organized around rail service to the city and region. A two-level roadway connects a new ground transportation center to Terminals 1 and 2. The design of the new terminal captures the spirit of the Harbin region, famous for winter sports and festivals, and transforms the airport into a world-class gateway. One critical issue Gensler confronted was the future of air travel. The design has the flexibility to allow the airport to grow incrementally as passenger demand increases and to accommodate innovations in aircraft and technology.

OPPOSITE •• **The ticketing hall makes abundant use of natural light as a design element. The open plan makes it easy for the airport to change furnishings and equipment without major reconstruction.**

Nicknamed the "Ice City," Harbin's Ice and Snow Festival attracts tourists from all over China. The terminal's design takes inspiration from large snow sculptures, with roof forms that appear to be shaped naturally by the wind. The tapered cylindrical control tower is the focal point of twin entry roads flanking a reflecting pool, adorned with ice sculptures in winter. On the interior, references to the cold climate contrast with accents of warm colors and materials. Red, the color of celebration and hospitality in China, balances forms and patterns signifying ice and snow.

Gensler designed the new terminal as a set of fully choreographed experiences that allow each traveler to feel like an important person, not an anonymous one in a large crowd. Forming a sophisticated landmark, the terminal is a grand, modern facility that show-cases Harbin's place in the world.

Departing passengers have a choice of intuitive self-service or highly personalized full service. Security is fast and efficient. Once through security, travelers have an immediate place to regroup before moving to the gates. The airside dining and shopping areas draw on Harbin's distinctive culture and cuisine. Once they reach the departure lounge, passengers find a variety of settings and activities, depending on their circum-stances. There are places to read quietly, places to have a light snack or a drink, and even a playground for young children. In each case, the gates are in view. Arriving passengers are similarly welcomed with an image consistent with the city and its attractions. And transit to Harbin-area destinations is close at hand.

Section View

1: Departures concourse
2: Ticketing
3: Departures
4: Arrivals corridor
5: Baggage-claim
6: Arrivals

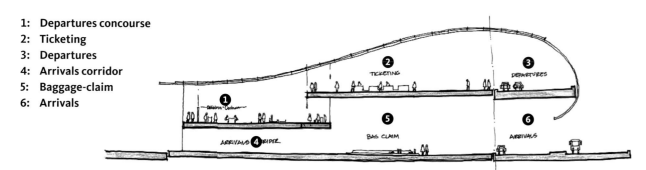

Sustainability is an important part of Gensler's strategy for the airport's modernization. A variety of approaches are employed. Daylight, filtered to prevent glare, supplements artificial lighting on the interior. High walls help bounce natural light to the passenger areas. Large air ducts deliver conditioned air to these spaces at a low velocity, reducing the power demand.

Harbin Taiping International Airport exemplifies an important new category in international aviation: gateway airports that connect their cities and regions to even bigger international hub airports that are a considerable source of their passenger traffic.

ABOVE ●● **The new terminal is sustainably designed to provide a high standard of peformance, both in the efficiency of its operation and in the quality of the indoor environment. Access to natural light and views gives arriving travelers an immediate sense of place and orients every passenger within the space.**

Detroit Metropolitan Airport

**North Terminal Replacement
Romulus, Michigan, USA**

In brief

A three-level, 26-gate terminal that serves domestic and international flights. The linear plan results in a compact profile that speeds passenger flow and airplane turnarounds.

Metropolitan Detroit's gateway, the 850,000-square-foot, 26-gate North Terminal serves some 12 million domestic and international passengers per year. Taking advantage of a narrow site, its glass-and-steel volume has a muscular presence that reflects the city's industrial heritage. One of the most cost-effective post-9/11 terminals in the US, the North Terminal's ticketing, security, and boarding areas are designed to let the airport make changes overnight instead of requiring weeks. Its efficient planning gets passengers quickly to their gates and shortens the taxiing time for aircraft, reducing emissions and fuel consumption. Highly sustainable, the terminal even reduces the energy consumption of aircraft at its gates.

OPPOSITE ●● **The escalator from the baggage-claim level, showing a detail of the terminal's main façade.**
OVERLEAF ●● **The terminal from the arrival road.**

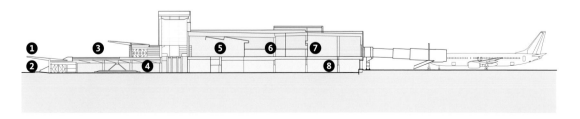

Terminal Cross-Section

1: Existing bridge
2: Arrivals area
3: Departure level
4: Baggage claim
5: Ticketing
6: Passenger checkpoint
7: Concourse
8: Baggage handling

0   30   60   120 ft

OPPOSITE •• Major circulation paths are given a strong visual interest by the rhythmic pattern of the floor, the walls, the signage, the open ceiling structure and lighting, and the vertical markers that signal approaching passages and crossings.

On the landside, the North Terminal appears as an extruded glass box. The steel-truss structure, visible behind the 660-foot-long curtain wall, gives it a robust industrial feeling. The linear, three-level plan, a function of the narrow site, makes passenger movement through the terminal very efficient.

On the airside, the gates can accommodate a range of aircraft sizes and are spaced to allow aircraft to maneuver easily. The terminal's narrow section also simplifies baggage handling. Immigration on the baggage-claim level serves international passengers. Modular components and raised floors in the security areas let the terminal change overnight, if necessary, to accept new equipment and uses.

Design fact

Length of the landside curtain wall

660 ft

Green fact

Value of FAA VALE Grant (see pg. 98)

$5.1 m

One design driver was ease of use. To help passengers find their way, the straightforward plan is reinforced with color cues at key transition points. This begins at the entry, denoted by a bright wall of transparent blue glass. Changing ceiling heights and lighting mark new settings. Sustainability also drove design. Only 15 percent of the building envelope is glass, but daylight reaches every level. The boarding bridges bring power, preconditioned air, and drinking water to parked aircraft. The linear plan allows aircraft to come and go without delay. They spend less time at the terminal and taxiing. This saves fuel, cuts emissions, and creates healthier working conditions on the apron. The terminal's holistic approach to sustainability, extending beyond its footprint, earned Detroit a $5.1 million Voluntary Airport Low Emissions grant from the FAA.

ABOVE, CLOCKWISE FROM TOP •• The security area has a wide portal to speed the screening process. The use of special lighting, blue-metal walls, and wood helps orient passengers as they cross the terminal. The baggage-claim level also houses international arrival facilities. **OPPOSITE** •• On the airside, food and beverage areas enjoy panoramic views. The exposed structure and ductwork save materials, part of the sustainability strategy.

Jomo Kenyatta International Airport

**New Gateway Terminal Complex
Nairobi, Kenya**

In brief

A design-build proposal for a new terminal that will enhance JKIA's status as the gateway airport to East Africa. The sustainable design takes full advantage of Nairobi's benign climate.

OPPOSITE •• **The main approach to the new terminal, with the "shield" as its centerpoint. Gensler's design for JKIA's modernization makes the lush greenery of the Nairobi area a landscape/roofscape feature.**

Gensler's proposed new terminal at Jomo Kenyatta International Airport (JKIA) supports the Kenyan capital's position as the gateway to East Africa and the region's prime tourist hub. The design-build modernization project, a partnership with Larsen & Toubro, is cost-effective, civic-minded, and sustainable. It will more than double the existing terminal's size and passenger volume, providing a distinctive passenger experience. Taking its cue from Kenya's stunning natural landscape, the terminal makes generous use of the outdoors to reduce the need for enclosed and conditioned interiors. The entry plaza, where people can congregate and socialize, is an example. A civic gesture, it welcomes travelers to the airport and provides a landscaped outdoor setting for its hotel.

Almost half of JKIA's travelers are transit passengers. Knowing that the airport will give them their main impression of Kenya, Gensler designed the shield to give hotel guests stimulating views of the plaza and the surrounding landscape. The shield is part of a retail and hotel complex that frames the terminal's roadside approach. Gently curving green roofs and berms give it prominence and relate it to the Kenyan landscape. The complex will provide the airport with an important source of revenue. Once inside the terminal, travelers can make a relaxed progression toward their gates. Concourse nodes are designed as calm settings, highlighted by double-height, glazed courtyards that open to the sky, bringing daylight, ventilation, and lush vegetation into the interior.

ABOVE ●● Passengers in transit can experience the Kenyan landscape in the garden courts that are a feature of the terminal. **OPPOSITE ●●** The shield, an element of the new airport hotel, gives the terminal an iconic focal point, visible from the garden plazas that adjoin it on both sides.

Site Plan

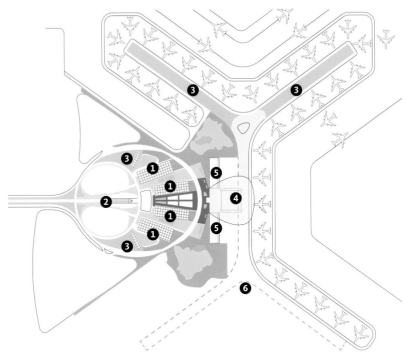

1: Hotel and retail
Landside location
fanned around terminal

2: Train station
Located on the center-
line of terminal

3: Landscaping
Green roofs and local
sourcing of plantings

4: The shield
Main hub contains
security screening

5: Arrival and departure
Contains baggage claim

6: Phase 2 expansion
Would double terminal
capacity going forward

Designed to function as wayfinding elements, the concourse courtyards also give waiting passengers a place of respite from surrounding activity. When open to the concourse, they serve as convection chimneys that help to naturally ventilate the adjoining space.

The terminal concourse is designed for incremental future growth with the addition of a southern wing and the expansion of hold-room size, strategies that offer a fine-tuned response to the client's desire for long-term resource- and cost-efficiency.

ABOVE ●● **The post-security walk to the marketplace gives travelers a panoramic airside view. Beyond is one of the outdoor terraces serving the restaurants.** OPPOSITE ●● **The airside concourses weave in views of the Kenyan landscape to create a sense of place.**

Corpus Christi International Airport

Replacement Terminal
Corpus Christi, Texas, USA

In brief

The phased redevelopment of a 1958 terminal, accomplished while the airport stayed in full operation. The distinctive waveform motif picks up on Corpus Christi's "City of Wind" image.

As the opening phase of a long-range modernization plan for the airport, Gensler designed the full-scale rebuild of a 1958 terminal, replacing 95 percent of its existing structure while the airport stayed in operation with a full flight schedule. The replacement terminal, with seven new gates, features a distinctive waveform roof that evokes Corpus Christi's Gulf Coast setting and seaside lifestyle. Gensler incorporated part of the existing terminal in the expansion and also recycled the existing terminal's structural steel for the new terminal's curbside canopy and renovated central concourse.

OPPOSITE •• The new terminal's signature waveform is immediately conveyed to arriving passengers by a canopy that invokes the nearby Gulf of Mexico surf.

To reinforce Corpus Christi as a tourist destination, the city asked Gensler to design a modern terminal to replace the 1958-era terminal's "dark, dingy confines." To keep the airport in operation, Gensler planned and orchestrated a six-phase renovation that retained elements of the old terminal. The essentially new building came in $2 million under budget, despite a redesign to meet changing security requirements.

Corpus Christi is known as the "City of Wind," and the terminal's waveform roof and entry canopy reflect this, providing visitors with a memorable image. Inside, travelers find a generous space, filled with natural light, art, and amenities, with an expanded food court and retail marketplace. The new terminal substantially shortens the walking distance from front door to gates. Parking is also closer and more convenient. In all, the airport gained 5,000 square feet of space and 578 more parking spaces, with new gates that can handle larger planes and more frequent flights.

Design fact

Airport capacity after modernization

7 gates

ABOVE •• The "Gulf wave" design of the canopy is set off against the simpler form of the terminal roof. **OPPOSITE, FROM TOP ••** Parts of the 1958 terminal were incorporated in the landside ticketing hall. Vertically separating security screening speeds departure and keeps the landside uncluttered.

Portland International Jetport

Airport Expansion
Portland, Maine, USA

In brief

An example of the new generation of smaller, high-performance terminals that capture the look and feel of their communities in a modern, sustainable, and passenger-friendly package.

Exemplifying "think global, act local," the expanded Portland International Jetport prioritizes sustainability, local building traditions, and the traveler's experience to support passengers and the planet. Built for high performance, the project incorporates a geothermal climate control system, Maine's largest, that will save $6.5 million over its life and reduce oil consumption by 50,000 gallons per year while delivering comfortable temperatures in every season. The exposed ceiling, designed to recall local shipbuilding, is made with Forest Stewardship Council (FSC)-certified products. The open interior orients passengers, brings in daylight, and creates an inviting evening destination. Passenger flow is served by a new ticketing hall, three new gates, and a spacious new security checkpoint.

OPPOSITE •• The beautifully designed and detailed wood roof, which shows off the traditional craft of Portland shipmakers, conveys pride of place as well as a sense of arrival befitting a regional gateway. **OVERLEAF** •• The airside entry sequence makes it easy for travelers to anticipate their next moves.

Portland International Jetport's expansion speaks to growing passenger demand. Reflecting Maine's allure as a year-round travel destination, the 137,000-square-foot project is state of the art, yet its design recalls the Pine Tree State's history of shipbuilding and stewardship. On track for LEED Gold certification, the Jetport is the first commercial terminal to tap a federal Voluntary Airport Low Emissions (VALE) grant. That paid for a geothermal climate control system with 23 miles of pipes and 120 ground wells buried 500 feet underground. The system delivers comfortable indoor air at half the cost of a conventional HVAC system.

The Jetport's exposed, FSC-certified wood ceiling is a reminder of Portland's shipbuilding prowess. To help travelers navigate, the terminal is open to light and views. A spacious security checkpoint, one level above the ticketing hall, relieves the stress of that process. Post-security, travelers regroup in an area where they also refill their water bottles. The deplaning sequence similarly makes exiting the airport fast and easy for its many passengers: 1.8 million in 2011.

BELOW •• The new Jetport's retail program speaks to Maine's perennial popularity as a tourist destination. **OPPOSITE ••** A grand stairway leads to the security checkpoint upstairs. The roof columns are both functional and iconic. **OVERLEAF ••** The clarity of the new Jetport is especially evident at night. The combination of transparency and strong forms gives it visual punch and a welcoming warmth.

Greater Lagos International Airport

New Gateway International Airport
Lagos–Ibadan Metroplex, Nigeria

In brief

A new international gateway airport for the Nigerian capital region, to be developed by a public-private consortium. The Gensler plan foresees an airport city growing up around it.

With the continued growth of the Lagos region and a likely shortage of facilities for next-generation aircraft, Nigeria's Ogun State and Heritage Aviation established a public-private consortium to develop a new gateway international airport equidistant to Lagos and Ibadan, planned and designed by Gensler. Accessible from the expressway linking the two cities, the new gateway will anchor an airport city by 2040, built in phases as a new regional hub for business, shopping, and tourism. The international terminal's soaring canopy sets the tone for the larger development with a powerful unifying image that suits the culture and climate, meets the consortium's performance and cost parameters, and provides air travelers to the capital region with a world-class standard of ambience and amenities.

OPPOSITE •• The canopy is a unifying element for the terminal, sheltering arriving passengers from the sun. OVERLEAF •• The canopy gives the airport a modern appearance that is rooted in the climate and culture of Lagos, Ibadan, and their region.

119

Site Plan

1: Cargo
2: Aircraft maintenance
3: General aviation
4: Fuel farm
5: Airport support office
6: Airport city
7: Rail link
8: Convention center
9: Hotel
10: Parking garage
11: Retail
12: Passenger terminal
13: Long-term parking
14: Cell phone lot
15: Commercial vehicle lot
16: Fire and police station
17: Air traffic control tower

OPPOSITE •• The new gateway is planned for phased expansion. It will also anchor related development, including a hotel, a conference center, and other uses. **OVERLEAF ••** A public garden plaza provides a gathering place for travelers and meeters-greeters.

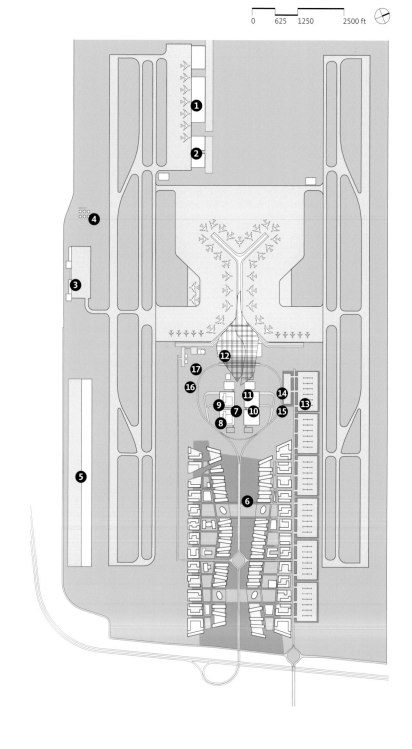

Design fact

Planned number of gates

55

Green facts

Light and translucent element of the canopy

Number of layers of the canopy system

ETFE | 3

The design reflects the airport's environmental and social context. The canopy is on a northeast-southwest axis to best capture rainwater and prevailing winds and protect passengers from the hot sun. The translucent canopy, made of ethylene tetrafluoroethylene (ETFE) for lightness, extends from the airport roadway to the concourse, allowing the different terminal buildings to function as independent elements that can be easily expanded without disrupting adjacent operations. At the terminal entry, adjacent to retail, conference, and hotel facilities, the canopy defines and shades a public garden plaza where visitors can shop and mingle. From there, passengers enter the terminal, pass through security, and move on to their gates.

Patterned paving guides passengers from the plaza to a concrete-and-glass ticketing pavilion, which connects to the airside concourse through a security checkpoint flanked by exterior gardens. Post-security, the terminal opens out to a central hold room and marketplace that recreates, on a smaller scale, the experience of the public garden plaza. Here, a three-story atrium brings daylight and greenery into the heart of the terminal, enhancing the passengers' preflight experience. The use of a centralized call-to-gate system saves space and cost by eliminating the need for individual hold rooms. It's also convenient. Waiting passengers can see and directly access concessions, which will maximize revenues for the airport's retail tenants.

Jackson Hole Airport

Terminal Renovation and Expansion
Jackson, Wyoming, USA

In brief

A modern riff on Wyoming's heritage, the airport now has the capacity to meet the peak demand of winter and summer tourism and the ongoing needs of the western state's gateway airport.

Jackson Hole Airport has a peak demand of 800 passengers per hour, befitting the gateway to a renowned leisure destination. Located in a national park, with stunning airside views of the Grand Teton mountain range, the airport made sustainability a high priority. Energy and water conservation, reuse of the existing structure, and no additional site impact were among the goals for the terminal's expansion, to be achieved while substantially increasing the airport's size and capacity. While the Jackson community sought regional resonance in the new terminal, it preferred a modern rather than a traditional style.

OPPOSITE •• Heavy timbers and crafted metal are the tradition-derived vocabulary for a modern terminal with a basic simplicity that defers to Jackson Hole's remarkable natural setting.

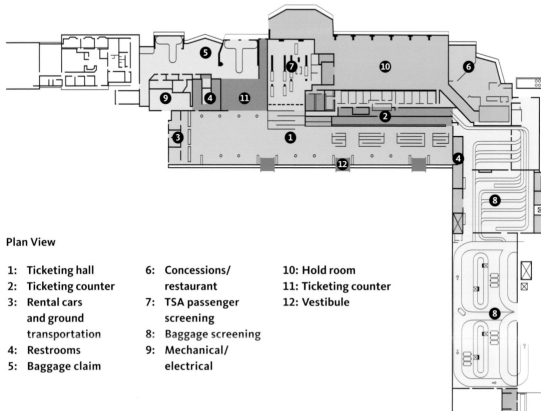

Plan View

1: Ticketing hall
2: Ticketing counter
3: Rental cars and ground transportation
4: Restrooms
5: Baggage claim
6: Concessions/ restaurant
7: TSA passenger screening
8: Baggage screening
9: Mechanical/ electrical
10: Hold room
11: Ticketing counter
12: Vestibule

OPPOSITE •• **The airside is anchored by a western-style lounge. ABOVE •• The blank wall outside the baggage-handling area is activated with stonework and native plants. OVERLEAF •• The terminal's low profile makes the Grand Tetons the main event.**

Teaming with local architects Carney Logan Burke and structural engineers Martin/Martin, Gensler planned the expansion to reuse 80 percent of the existing terminal structure and reclaim a parking lot. This made it possible to nearly double the size of the terminal without additional site impact. A more efficient building envelope and daylight sensors cut energy costs by 18 percent—with 70 percent use of green power. Water-efficient fixtures reduced building water use by 51 percent; using native landscaping and sustainable irrigation cut site potable water use by 64 percent. Recycled, reused, and regionally sourced materials and products were used extensively, and 94 percent of construction waste was reclaimed.

To keep the airport in operation, the expansion was carried out in two phases, first adding a new ticketing hall and in-line checked baggage system, and then remodeling the security checkpoint and inbound baggage area, renovating and expanding the holding area, and adding a new gate area and restaurant. Jackson Hole Airport experiences dramatic swings in demand—from 10,000 to 50,000 enplanements per month. To meet peak demand, the new ticketing hall was finished for the 2010 summer season (July and August); the renovation enlarged the hall and increased its ticket counters from 21 to 36.

Inside and out, the designers make constant reference to Jackson Hole as a place and a community. The building's modern vocabulary references the forms and materials of mountain architecture without any hint of kitsch or historicism. The daylight-filled interior affords constant views of the town's remarkable setting. Much of the furniture is sourced locally or regionally and made by local artisans. A 300-foot blank wall along the baggage-handling building is finished with rock ledges and rusted metal panels. The landscaping and planting reflect the microclimates of the town and the surrounding mountains.

John Wayne Airport

Airport Renovation and Expansion
Santa Ana, California, USA

In brief

The final phase of a regional airport that Gensler planned from the start, adding a third terminal and parking structure. The result is a high-tech airport that can handle international flights.

Gensler has been engaged for more than two decades in the expansion of John Wayne Airport, the gateway to Orange County, a popular destination for business and tourism in Southern California. The latest phase, completed in 2011, is the county's largest-ever public works project. It includes upgrades to the original, Gensler-designed Terminals A and B complex, a new parking structure for 2,024 cars, and a third terminal, the 282,000-square-foot Terminal C, which provides six additional passenger gates, including new federal passport control and inspection facilities for international arrivals. The airport's embrace of technology, allowing passengers to check in at any kiosk, makes it a bellwether project for the industry.

OPPOSITE •• **Terminal C brings forward the airport's signature barrel-arched roofs. OVERLEAF** •• **On the landside, the ticketing hall uses the barrel arch to make wayfinding simple and intuitive. The kiosks are universal, allowing passengers to get boarding passes from any airline that serves the airport.**

Security Entrance
Boarding Pass Required

135

Terminal C gave John Wayne Airport the opportunity to meet the highest standards of passenger comfort, improving on a passenger experience that was already very successful. Terminal C also fills gaps in service to Orange County, a leading West Coast destination. New US Customs and Border Protection and Federal Inspection Service facilities at Terminal C allow international flights. Besides adding six new gates and state-of-the-art baggage handling, the new terminal more than doubles the size of airport concessions.

Terminal C is especially notable for using technology to ensure a seamless passenger experience. Any kiosk can be used to check in for any flight on any airline, saving departing passengers the trouble of locating the "right" kiosk. The gates are also "neutral," giving the airport flexibility in allocating them to the airlines. High-tech solutions make Terminal C hospitable. The vaulted ceilings are evenly illuminated by LEDs, which use half the energy of metal halide lights and deliver improved color. Insulated windows cut cooling loads. Curved walls and Vierendeel-truss seismic bracing distinguish Terminal C from its predecessor.

ABOVE, TOP •• View of the tarmac from the airside.
ABOVE, BOTTOM •• Detail of the universal kiosk.
OPPOSITE •• The baggage claim provides art and attractiveness, a hallmark of John Wayne Airport.

Lisbon International Airport

New Gateway International Airport
Lisbon Metroplex, Portugal

In brief

A proposal for a new gateway airport in Portugal. Designed for a competition, it explored many of the ideas about the 21st-century airport that Gensler is implementing in other countries.

For an international design competition, Gensler developed an extensive proposal to address Portugal's ambition to build a new international gateway airport. Due to the limited capacity of the current Lisbon Airport and barriers to significant expansion there, the new facility will occupy a 7,500-hectare site 42 kilometers east of central Lisbon—creating, in Gensler's vision, the infrastructure for a transit-based airport city. The new airport's terminal has a streamlined look that captures the thrill of flight at the moment of liftoff. Experientially, the terminal is designed as an extension of Lisbon itself, a network of gardens and interior spaces that reference the city's tradition of urban parks and plazas. The design integrates environmental, social, and economic aspects of the city to create a memorable and sustainable whole.

OPPOSITE ●● Airside amenities reflect Lisbon's many public gathering places in spirit. **ABOVE ●●** Art and form create a promenade experience for passengers as they walk to their flights.

By organizing the new terminal around a transportation center that provides a direct rail connection to the heart of Lisbon, Gensler's design establishes the framework for a vibrant airport city that can evolve and grow over time. The new airport is organized around a central corridor that leads to the core of the transportation center, which accommodates a rail terminal, bus station, rental car facilities, taxi staging, and short-term parking. The rail terminal is the center's nucleus, with three 200-meter-long platforms that are sheltered by a glass-and-steel canopy. The second-level retail and restaurant hub, organized around a series of outdoor courtyards, will also provide access to future airport hotels.

The terminal design focuses on comfort and efficiency of movement for passengers, flexibility to accommodate physical and functional changes over the long term, sustainability of energy and operating costs, and satisfaction of the airport's business goals. A detailed statistical analysis of passenger characteristics informed the programming and planning phase. Using annual enplanement statistics, Gensler defined various types of air travelers based on their use of the airport. Designing for their needs ensured a stress-free environment that encourages their loyalty. A large central marketplace serves as the heart of the new airport, a sumptuous place to shop and dine while waiting for flights.

Green fact

Sensitive environment preserved

1,000 ha

OPPOSITE •• The new airport's greenfield site allows constant views of the surrounding landscape. **ABOVE** •• At full development, the airport will incorporate a variety of related uses. **OVERLEAF** •• The airport is directly accessible from Lisbon by intercity trains.

At Lisbon, Gensler took a unique approach to integrating the manmade environment with its natural surroundings, capitalizing on the opportunity to set a new standard for ecological stewardship. While large airports traditionally isolate travelers from the outdoors for both security and pragmatic reasons, Lisbon International Airport connects travelers to the surrounding natural landscape. Yet the terminal is sited so that the larger natural settings are minimally disturbed, with more than 1,000 hectares of sensitive environment preserved. A natural buffer zone between these settings and the airport runways keeps waterborne and airborne pollutants to a minimum.

Palm Springs International Airport

Airport Expansion
Palm Springs, California, USA

In brief

A benign desert climate made possible the use of a tent-like roof to shelter the airport's largest concourse and the walkways. Every aspect of the expansion takes advantage of the outdoors.

In 1964, Palm Springs revived a shuttered World War II Army airfield as its airport. Over the last decade, Gensler's phased expansion of the airport cemented the city's stature as one of America's premier desert resorts, giving it the capacity to handle future passenger growth. Two new concourses added a total of 16 gates and an array of concessions. The concourses connect to the original terminal, newly renovated by Gensler, by covered walkways. Palm Springs has a desert climate with warm and sunny days in midwinter and cool nights even in the summer. This gave the design team a rare opportunity to design the concourses with the natural environment of the surrounding Coachella Valley in mind.

OPPOSITE •• At dusk and at night, the tent structure of the concourse roof is a well-loved landmark in Palm Springs. ABOVE •• The outdoors is an integral part of the passenger experience.

145

OPPOSITE, TOP •• **The translucent roof filters the sunlight in the agora-like courtyard of the main concourse.** OPPOSITE, BOTTOM •• **Outdoor terraces are provided.** RIGHT •• **Palm Springs' lifestyle is integral to the experience.** OVERLEAF •• **The San Jacinto Mountains form a dramatic background.**

The area's warm and sunny climate suggested tents as the ideal means to enclose the main passenger areas. A staple of hot, arid regions the world over, tents offer shade and shelter while letting in light and air. For the concourses and their connecting walkways, Gensler designed tents of lightweight, cable-supported Teflon. Each of the concourses' large tents has a dome-shaped, vented cap to pull hot air from the interior by convection. The tents are inherently energy-efficient and cost-effective to operate. While the concourses are air-conditioned on the hottest summer days, the tents keep them comfortably cool the rest of the year. Thanks to their distinctive appearance, the tents have become a symbol of Palm Springs as a desert paradise.

Plan

1: Drop-off curb
2: Main entry
3: Ticketing wing
4: Security checkpoint
5: Outdoor courtyard
6: Bono concourse
7: Commuter terminal hold room
8: Baggage claim
9: Concessions
10: Restrooms

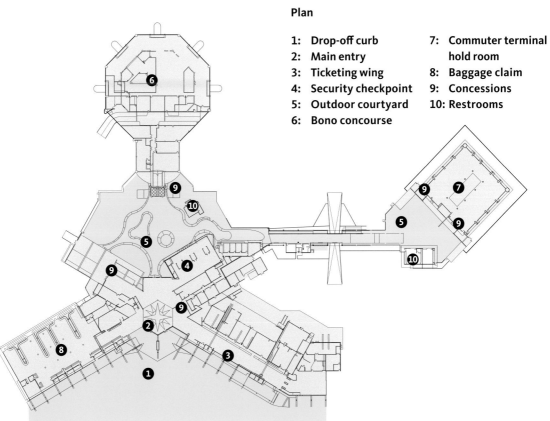

Index

Image credits

All images credited to Gensler unless otherwise noted.

Aker/Kvonkovic: pages 107-108
Atort Photography: page 93
Robert Benson: pages 110-117
Bruce Damonte: page ii, right; page 10, bottom
Ryan Gobuty/Gensler: pages 144-149
Tim Griffith: pages 128-129; page 132; pages 134-137
Mori Hidetaka: page ii, left; page 2; pages 12-13;
    page 33; pages 36-37
JetBlue: page 48, image 5
John Wayne Airport: page 133
David Joseph: page 98, top and bottom right; page 99;
    page 109
Nic Lehoux; page i; pages 4-6; pages 42-45; page 48,
    image 2, 3, and 6; pages 50-54; page 55, top; page 58,
    top left, bottom left and right; pages 59-61
John Edward Linden: page 8
Nick Merrick/Hedrich Blessing : page 15
Matthew Millman: inside front cover; page 9; page 127;
    pages 130-131
Vito Palmisano: pages 94-96, page 98, bottom left
Prakash Patel: back cover; page 40; pages 46-47; page 48,
    image 1
Frank Pinckers: inside back flap; page 30; page 32;
    pages 34-35; pages 38-39
Sherman Takata: front cover; pages 16-17; pages 63-66
Adrian Wilson: page 48, image 4

The LEED Certification Mark is a registered trademark owned by the U.S. Green Building Council and is used by permission.

Inside back cover, from left: Changi Airport Singapore Terminal 2, Portland International Jetport. Back cover: John F. Kennedy International Airport JetBlue Terminal 5.